Night said

Mary Burritt Christiansen Poetry Series

HILDA RAZ,
Series Editor

The Mary Burritt Christiansen Poetry Series publishes two to four books a year that engage and give voice to the realities of living, working, and experiencing the West and the Border as places and as metaphors. The purpose of the series is to expand access to, and the audience for, quality poetry, both single volumes and anthologies, that can be used for general reading as well as in classrooms.

Also available in the Mary Burritt Christiansen Poetry Series:

Punishment Bag: Poems by Jake Fournier
Midsummer Count: New and Selected Poems by Robin Becker
a chronology of blood: poems by Teo Shannon
small lives: poems by Gary Jackson
A Real Man Would Have a Gun: Poems by Stacey Waite
Dream of the Bird Tattoo: Poems and Sueñitos by Juan J. Morales
Unruly Tree: Poems by Leslie Ullman
A Walk with Frank O'Hara: Poems by Susan Aizenberg
Light of Wings: Poems by Sarah Kotchian
Trials and Tribulations of Dirty Shame, Oklahoma: And Other Prose Poems by Sy Hoahwah

For additional titles in the Mary Burritt Christiansen Poetry Series, please visit unmpress.com.

University of
New Mexico
Press

Albuquerque

Night said

Poems

Barbara Rockman

Printed in the United States of America

Library of Congress Cataloging-in-Publication Data
Names: Rockman, Barbara, 1949– author
Title: Night said / Barbara Rockman.
Other titles: Mary Burritt Christiansen poetry series (bcp47)
Description: Albuquerque : University of New Mexico Press, 2026. | Series: Mary Burritt Christiansen poetry series
Identifiers: LCCN 2026013682 | ISBN 9780826370136 paperback | ISBN 9780826370143 epub
Subjects: BISAC: POETRY / American / General | POETRY / Women Authors | LCGFT: Poetry
Classification: LCC PS3618.O35447 N54 2026
LC record available at https://lccn.loc.gov/2026013682

Founded in 1889, the University of New Mexico sits on the traditional homelands of the Pueblo of Sandia. The original peoples of New Mexico—Pueblo, Navajo, and Apache—since time immemorial have deep connections to the land and have made significant contributions to the broader community statewide. We honor the land itself and those who remain stewards of this land throughout the generations and also acknowledge our committed relationship to Indigenous peoples. We gratefully recognize our history.

Cover and frontispiece photograph by Janet Russek
Designed by Isaac Morris
Composed in Centaur MT

Contents

I

II

III

IV

Aftermath

I

Night said

Travel small

No documents of calamity
No passport stamped   *plague and plea*
No exclamation points   one question

You've been given an occluded moon
to learn how to hide and how to slide
from hiding

Loose weave   cloud lace
too thin a comfort to sleep beneath
What will come of waiting?

Cramped   calloused
and swollen feet
by dirt and dew   will soften

On her stone step   the black dog curls
Tail twitch   only sign she dreams

Beneath and behind
loved ones sleep

You cease to carry each
overpacked valise

There was   pause

and the humans were afraid
and grasses in the meadow
were still

and hawks who loved
to hunt small creatures
circled.

Pews   barren of bodies
infected with yesterday's prayers
exhaled.

Frayed with bewilderment
hymnals released a scent of sorrow
and what had not been memorized
stayed shut.

Outside the open door   beyond
the worn stone steps
air moved.   Birds

blustery with spring lust
ransacked back lots and alleys for
sticks and dead grass.

Humans   so hidden
it was as if   cloud and root and hill
demanded

    Stay back   stay away   stay in.
    Face your smeared windows
    your unread holy texts.

There will be rearrangement
of angels   animals   and humankind—
order inclined toward   insect   ocean   and oak.

Reckon with and return
when you have learned
tiferet   *chesed.*

Then   open your door
curl your shoulders down
walk   as it is commanded by beast
and breeze and blue black dusk

into remnants   of holiness   and grace

God in the Lesser Nighthawk

chordeiles, n. evening dance with music; Gr. person who
prefers to be awake at night

Insomniac in search of respite,
my red-eyed dog and I go into the field

. . . star bright, first star I see tonight . . .
I think if I distract God,

change my plea from ethereal to mundane,
I will catch Her Holiness off guard.

I wish for *Chordeiles acutipennis* to swoop
moonbeam to porch light.

I'd been researching night birds but
nary nightjar nor goatsucker blessed the sky

though there were moths and humming.
It was summer. Grass crunched.

Eggs had been laid in scars left by fires.
I treaded carefully, fearful

I'd crush the unhatched on blistered paths.
I imagined the hawk's bristled gape,

tremolo and keen, white striped wings
glowing like plane lights—ever-hungry forager

as I, night after night, crave heaven's feast
but am offered star thorns and breeze.

I turned to the earthbound herding dog
curved to my thigh.

No avian eye shine. No whine or dive.
No evening song with strings.

Back Pain

After multiple healings
—hot stones and liniment,
stranger's hands kneading spine and hips,

the angel spoke,

Go naked.
Rest upon a snowfield.

After months of drought, the frozen earth was given
barely enough snow to hide stabs of grass.

Fall onto your knees once the moon has peaked.
Eye to eye with snow-creased trunks.

Lie back. Read each celestial letter.

I winced onto brittle crust.

No deep powder, girlhood
arms and legs flapping angel gown and wings.

No moonlit drifts I leapt and rolled
plundering the pristine.

My black dog stood by.

I lay still   opened my palms
and swallowed.

Planets were intermittent
the way a neon sign blinks in intervals   requires we accumulate
and recall words to complete its message.

And the angel lulled   *Rise*

My shepherd pried me to stand as if
I were a lamb strayed from its mother.

We were returned to
copper windows   common rooms—

High Summer's Thin Wrist

Dark moon. Pulling weeds I name *crisp mallow*
cave-bent *gorge dive* *hell-bent-for-heaven*
ploved and plundered *shear sorrow*

I am not better than what invades my fable—
yard I made from dust, tumbleweed, and hollow cactus.
Where I once dreamt succulence and a barefoot blend

now a third dog tugs a luminous bone—
or root or is it shadow confused with treasure
buried in hillocks blind beasts sponge beneath our feet?

Cicadas scream. Rodents spit seed hulls.
Moon twisted from its buttonhole is lost in creases—
mine and drought-ruined earth's.

Who are we stripped down to our unrocked bodies?
Buxom Giver of Life, dance me to the center
of this hacked, gasping land.

I'll pull invasive rhymes: *evacuate* *placate* *ingrate.*
You, plant tunes even the tone deaf,
even the mongrel, can carry.

At the Burren Craft Fair, I Search a Sign

The jeweler crafted a tiny concertina
and soldered a silver bee   abdomen antennae and wings
atop buttons and bellows.

He split the instrument's hexagons
as if it were a cracked nut or locket
hollow where song or succor

might be saved—
charm to be hung
round neck or wrist.

    When I was a girl a bee walked the dock of my finger.
    I brought it to my ear to hear it hum. Did I think
    I would not be stung?

        My mother wore a golden bee on her lapel.
        My grandmother's locket keeps neither
        curl nor grainy girlhood.

What did the jeweler mean   *It's spells I'm after*
that the miniature instrument overseen
by a silver drone might wheeze lament

and inhale luck?

Night Child | *Woman* | *Once Girl* | *Dog* |

Confusion of Voices, Summer of Pandemic

Black dog and I go out
  Five a.m. dawn star reluctant to quit
  Rib thin and weak she carves her bone back to my bare calf

Blue black silhouettes— familiar ash and oak
turned foreign as if palm palmetto
shadows as if moss drift

I am not from here
Was it Woman's voice
Night Child Dog or Once Girl?

Beneath lilac into lily-of-the-valley
Once Girl crept every lily bell embossed to finger tip
The scent stayed white scent and plum-black lilac

Is it the darkest part of the story yet? Night Child asks
Will beast descend from stalk Will beauty be locked in glass
Will there be meal root cider Will the well be vermin or clear?

I am not from here
Once Girl says to tree fringe that shudders
so terribly small a shiver and then is stiller than

Dog pants drools presses for answers
There's paralysis Her throat stays wide when meant to shut
like the star that refuses to dim or the moon afloat at noon

Night Child twirls   swings thin arms
Her skirt stitched with milkweed
pods   split and plume

Swollen heart   bone ashimmer with
what might kill her   still she is
beyond prediction   Good Dog

Is there magic that lasts?
It is so slim   Night Child's voice
whisper of summer sweat

I am not sure   about quarantine   says Dog
It is hot   I am not well   the river I remember my paws
wet and cold   Can we

Swell but no thunder   brief breeze
Sleep—   a broken vessel   shards everywhere
Woman says   Be careful where you step

Tell a good ending   she says

Was it Dog or Woman who spoke
Once Girl or Night Child?

Gophered Night

Old stars planed their cataracts
shone down upon

me shivering in vest and hoodie too thin for winter
my black dog too head-down to gopher tunnel
to be claimed but I

felt ashamed   one among people
peeled back and seen
my mouth locked into repeating ". . . but what *I* need"

even as my feet loved freezing bristle beneath
as frost laced each nostril and coppered trees
crackled leaves   the dead twisted free

even as the gopher dug blind in my off-season
oft-forgotten garden   no   call it yard
for it was rough   untended

Call it earth   what I'm hurled against
and walled off from and fail to repair
Tikkun olam intone the rebbes

There was creaking in language I've learned poorly
It said   *Shame is not among our teachings*
but wonder is

My black dog unhooked her nose from dirt
pulled her legs back from crouch to stand and
I swear   she whinnied

What are we but
hush hollowed out
and its shed lining

Come   I called
Night sung

> *Bless everything of stars*
> *and far down deep down*
> *back down into kinship with*

but I was bundled against
as I often am   too stiff to respond

Bread in the Time of COVID-19

Spelt   levain   boule
cracked ark   golden yurt
baguette's bark canoe   challah's fat hips

Unbraid and eat
in a dark kitchen
in bed under cover   on the back step at dawn

It's relentless
craving   as if breast   as if moss and mountain
as if cool walking   pond and dew

Black bread of my ancestors   manna that bandages
banned *nonessential*   mold inducer
cause of the doughy midriff

Multi-seed and local   equal opportunity
factory-bagged and trucked cross-state
waited-in-line-for   neighbor-to-neighbor bread

Fill our rooms with rising
scent of a future   eyes closed   teeth into
Christ bread   Jehovah bread   bread of Allah

bread of children   bread of refusal
bread of my seclusion
and yours

Oh crust
tough as a belt that holds us together
crisp as ice that shatters into song

Yeast   water   salt
What Moses survived without
I am ravenous

Loaf of COVID   loaf of grief
loaf of what's offered and
what's stolen

May there be bread of a new year
challah round as a labyrinth
strewn with cinnamon and raisins

maze of our craving   bread
of our saving

Near Acre of Home

Dear dog who shoulders
ladders of night shadow so I might walk beneath

Apple and oak who
because the same hand planted you bicker as siblings

Dear sinking gate   despite warp and split
a latch that will not meet its other half   keeps out and lets in

snake   squirrel
mouse   wasp and hare   who tunnel and cling to

house of mud and pine
cracked tile   pecked stucco   windows that look out

and look in   to stove   ladle and spatula
pot and skillet   that steam and flip and fill

walls of books my mother read to me
that her mother read to her   that I read to my daughters

quilt   burrow   nest   dear dirt and down
soft bodies that curl and twitch

animal   earth   and ancestor

I lean against

Disturbed Pastoral

begins with rose light we sleep through
wake to seamlessness   white cloth settled
as if readying a summer feast

but it is not summer
nor is there food to feed length of a trestle table

By feed I mean   we are hungry
snow its own miracle of manna

Though look   already the dog
has spoiled it   so now allow
the sharp-shinned hawk

to tear prey from a low limb
press into white earth
the captured robin

Surely the hawk has punctured the breast
Wind unsettles his back   He does not look up

I cannot see how hard the talons work
or hear a death wheeze or feel
melting beneath

Then it is over
The hawk lifts   swerves   carries its kill

Evidence is delicate   a trail of blood stains
soft feathers like grass   ice-caught and wind-torn

And there   look
the whole tail   a fan
spread so I can study every overlap

every hue   how rust merges into black
black to gray   how each narrowing white tip
disappears against snow

Home Meadow

The first winter   before we imagined garden
before we fenced the first dog
before we walled ourselves against rabbits   coyote—

not yet familiar with this place
I mistook them for fallen trees—
deer lying on midnight snow

When one great head turned and then another
When I counted four resting so close I could call to them

I woke him   Moonlit   standing on cold tile
we held hands   The deer surveyed the snowfield

Decades later   spring of great fire   summer of rain
in daylight   we are visited by a thin one-antlered male

He is young and a metal barb cuts into
and cramps one ankle

How any of us are injured is mystery
how any of us are saved

He eats apples from the tree we planted twenty years ago
He shakes his half-horned head

and bounds   through asters   cactus   and ash

II

Deer in Closet   Hawk on Piñon Limb

Because three fawns stand in a dreamt closet
we are told to circumvent   as, *use the roundabout*
to leave the stranger's house—

I believe in dappled fur and spindly legs
as some believe in wafers set to melt upon the tongue.
I want to be among the hibernating   the ruminant and hooved

to curl in grass pressed between boulders
to live out winter on frozen earth
in wind and sleet.

In the dream   my husband resists instruction to be
rerouted.   Stubborn   he wants to stay
to store data of the fawns' bodies.

> Is it sin to study rapid breath
> of a trapped beast? to not steady
> its quaking motherlessness?

Yesterday he beckoned me to watch
a hawk on a black-muscled piñon limb
bend to breakfast   tear feathers from a jay—

> Oh to rip and devour   gulp lung and bone
> To be feathers spit and pierced by cholla spears
> To be wind that riles wingtips stretched for departure

How bland my boxed and toasted meal

How I barely use my body

As Wildfire Spread, I Became a Jew

The sky was brown, July
but fireworks banned.

My inventory of black shirts
hung by sleeve length,
hung in one direction.

My metal boxes readied,
my cartons' yawning flaps.
        But, so tired—

    I dreamt those I loved
    turned to ash in their beds.

    Dreamt a pale boy deciphered
    the label on my pajamas:
    FLAMMABLE FABRIC

    It was the sleep of my ancestors rushing past.
    Everything they could carry in two suitcases,
    stars sewn to their breasts.

    Train fumes gagging the rails
    and every truck disgorging
    a rash of homelessness.

There was no retardant then.
No law stitched between seams
to protect the child.

No heroes dropping
foam onto forest tops nor those
who refused to evacuate—that luxury.

I grabbed every black shirt, every dark dress
clustered to my breast. Soon,
soon I will run.

Erev Shabbat, I Become Matriarch

Because days are long and daughters in far-off cities
Because times are dire   hope slim   sleep fitful
we fear our country's cruelties
we are lonely   two Jews
in a house too dark

I pull my grandmother's crooked candlesticks
from the cupboard   set them by the sink
The silver is thin   embossed with grape vines
With a white cloth   I clean tarnished crevices
With another   I buff to bright sheen

I rummage the drawer for tapers
shave and twist them to fit
turn the tilting and bent silver bases
so the grape-roped pedestals
are as even as they'll get

At sunset I ignite wicks   stand and
beckon light with open palms
What I have been awkward with I need
My mother is long dead

No one complains that we
say Sabbath prayers in language
more rhythm and blood than commitment

I do not bake but buy challah
Jewish husband and I tear into
there is no wine

and   yet   briefly
we are blessed and
enter briefly   rest

The Dead Imitate the Goldfinch

Days of Awe upon us and I have
yet to sidle up to the words of God.
But I swear this year I will unearth

my aunt's soup bowls
my grandmother's gold-leaf platter
burnish their necklaces

set them on the table to be filled.
The ash tree's leaves shudder and flick
scrape screens   so like yellow wings

I want my dead to slip through windows
though my mother had little to say
about faith and my father

would make of *finch* a winch
of *gold* a soldier
—a limerick to save us.

All summer I've waited for this
dying off—for my dead
to open coats and pull me in.

Renegade   refusenik   recluse
sprawl on their backs
to better scan the starscape

moan through centuries of thefts—
lace that tented challah
wheat-etched goblet

as the ash tree goldens
as aspens rattle and repent.

New Year's Beside the Playa

Great Basin, Oregon

This dry lake bed, big as the universe,
does not offer refuge: you have to make your own.

Sun just up and grief rises in alternating lines.
Old dirt stays under nails. My mother's digging.
My daughter's smashed castle.

Night wind stretched strings taut and didn't let go
and when it did: rubber bands snapped back to cheeks.

How fragile we are facing front
straight into the new season with no old markers.

Nothing weather-strips our crevices.
All the layers of wool won't shield us
from what slams our flimsy gates.

Our doors no match for animals that pace and growl,
wait until daybreak to push their tails and talons through
chinks we'll never putty up.

Frailty: our soft-boned destiny.
We spend lifetimes layering insulation,
talk and newsfeeds, somebody else's business.

Pond to sunrise, ducks lift their wavering V.
Shore's fanged grasses transform clench to yawn.

Why not? It's never the sleep of sweet dream;
nothing we can do to grip against failure.

Monday asks for no one's prayers, offers bird clatter but no wings.
Cloud called *Do not look me in the eye*
Cloud called *Comfort a mother cannot wrap round her daughter*

Afternoon rain natter and spurt, no true drenching.
But it is the new year and God is close:
rainbow over a snow-tricked playa,
sun on chewed grass.

The thing is: you stayed long enough to see it.

Girl with Red Scarf, Dreamt Tale

The child's cheeks flushed with winter
mottled ornaments once hooked to pine
Red boots Blue coat barrel buttons looped into wool

Do not follow the swap of starlings that swoop like half rinds
nor wind pressing grasses parallel to field

Follow a red scarf that whips her shoulders
tightens round her collar neck chafed rough red the cardinal placed

Blond curls escape a cap tied beneath her chin
Her eyes sky but not enemy blue

Tears freezing in rivulets
She is round in a flat field Snow as far as sky curves

I called to the girl

I wanted
to be her mother or I wanted
my mother's red scarf to fall from a closet shelf

to wrap my neck
with foreign hands that knotted the tassel
knit the red length that swung behind

My mother turned
the menorah's star to the wall
sang *and a partridge in a pear tree*

plump birds twelve days
but it was the wrong story

The girl reached back
did not remove her sodden mitten
tugged me into

a snowfield ruined with upturned pots
rotting stew   black leaves like scabs

Into frozen boot prints   we
two girls tripped and lifted

> Once I had a coat blue as paraffin the menorah dripped
> blue as egg and glass   as day's last shudder

> Do not clamor the fence lost in drifts
> nor enter the pasture soft with silence
> nor fall back to carve your angel

Stand between these stories:
Two girls   dusk burnished
bitten by icy air   grip wool-wet hands

> nor demand of your mother
> answers long lost beneath crust
> and creaks of a field you have not trespassed

In the Year of Much Winter and Men

Sodden   weight-in-the-gut morning
Bruise between digit and wrist
Bark riveted with sleet scabs

It is difficult to walk out

Fear of falling   For all its terrible
beauty   the dog returns flecked
with crystals   eyes crust-stuck with ice

We cannot return to sleep

Woman after woman
stomps her boots   demands to enter
solitude   misted pines

Men have ruined almost everything

but crossed black limbs   so like the puzzle a girl solves
braids shaken out   snow boughs released
animals crouch beneath

Frozen sap globs trunks

Oh   may tracks be girl knees pressed into
and risen   be finch claw   hare foot
black scat and cracked seed

Come world of tongues   knife-bite morning

so cold white   you'd think other than
invitation but oh   tart wit   brittle cry
it is a kneel-down   shatter song

Snowstorm with Lament

I am alive   strained pine boughs
locked in drifts   my daughter's
girlhood friend is dead

I wander all day   one window to next
glisten and harbor   snow folds its batting
Why now remember how the magpie

grieved its mate splayed on dirt
whipped its wingtips against   beating
love into   screamed its grating cry

Trill and chatter replaced by
fury   *How dare you*   shrills the widow
pecking pebbles as if to raise his breast

How can this loss be mine?
She bursts into nervous flight
inches above the body

Surely his beak will open hungry
surely another season   to migrate and settle
a brood   cloudless   pivot   and singing

but only a thin wind lifts the dead's feathers
only gravel and dust shift beneath

She leaves and returns with grasses
makes of her forage a bolster
twigs and dry weeds—

a grief wreath
a litter to slip under him as if
she might drag him to a better place

and through it all
the terrible shrieking plea

Raft Dress, Refugee

She spread paper   thin as an aerogram
Backlit   silhouetted her shape onto tissue   traced her shadow

Pinned to ripstop thick as rain   she sheared herself a size larger than
made its double: triple-stitched shoulder to shoulder

smeared Teflon to seams   The twin shapes would become
inflatable bed to hold her   Departure: packed with balsa and foam

A garment can withstand swell if the body
can withstand laceration   salt and purpling

Weeks she worked   before others rose
Under her pillow   the plosives that propelled her: *prosper plea*

She left   one cupboard flung wide   two cups   canister of tea
brothers   bed stripped to coils   receipt for needles thick as nails

In her skirt pocket: duct tape   nuts   her god   Her legs legend
on the sheep-mad hills   her body   a cage bundled against

The night she fled dragging the bigger-than shape of herself
down dust streets   One dog bared teeth   One bell clung to rust

She hefted the raft dress onto her back   knew which alley was least lit
Others had left a trail: cracked photos   burnt log

She reached an inlet   knelt and blew from a belly that had never held a child
blew into what she'd made   Tossing out onto low tide   dress she blessed

threw her body   onto slick rocking   Her dark hair flared
Her skirt: spread wings   Pushed off   paddled out   Surveillance might

identify *angel* or *pelagic bird*   Paddled and prayed   plosives
in her ear: *portal*   *plow*   *Do not prey upon*

Day night day over   moon   storm   wind like clamps to her breast
Her face salt-iced   legs numb   arms bandaged in kelp and gull shit

Air easing out   Dream was too heavy   Barely able when her face scratched beach
cyclone of tatters   Orange dye transferred to flesh   alarm

Shore of human leavings   hers   a shroud stumbling to stand
How old she appeared to those who salvaged her

January Morning, Poet Beholds One Leaf

Despite ice beneath
black stem latched to branch,
the brittle leaf cradles its mosaic map.

Copper canoe, frost crusted, brief,
rolls crystals tongue to teeth—

Be robin's breast.
Be ache between mountains.
Mirror my clawed spine.

Be leather pouch
filled with jacks and a red ball
smell of girlhood . . .

> boots crunching shirred pasture,
> bell bolted by the back door, my mother's hand
> about to grip the leather strip, hit the clapper, call me home.

Bright morning, frozen earth—
unfence my loneliness.
Invite me to belong.

Vulture hunkered to a high limb, bent *rebbe,*
hunched thug, priest caught in daydream—
be teacher, be rebel, be me.

May my tongue curl and funnel
notes to a song I've not been taught—
barks and caws, whinnies and brays.

May my hands be burnt to
ash of my mother's hands,
cold breath steaming toward prayer.

I mark in ink

cross hatch   mind ashevel   a shelf
from which fall socks and keys

crumpled print   smeared handkerchiefs
frayed cuffs   chipped cups   newspaper strips rolled into logs

I know nothing

Neither who I was before I slept
nor who I am in black slumber

I am writing my way into devotion
what a poet names awe   a storyteller insists is myth

I know nothing

Dear goddess of alphabets   hieroglyphs and lost
tunes my ancestors left throbbing in my neck

Let me be silent

Set me down on the lip of the stream
to study how ice bubbles breath into orbs

Show me how to ingest fists of snow   suck crystals
distill whiskey of what is wanted of me

But the winter day is uncannily warm
mountains barren of frost

Nowhere is Long Ago
woods smoky with lavender and umber nor
iced log I straddled   nor fox   hare
and witch   I conversed with there

Of bed and body   she neither made

nor can rest upon   She is   ill upon an ill land

The woman has taken to her bed
Her hips protest and upon her palm
a pebble embeds itself

Her throat   a riverbed gone narrow
inflected with others' sins
dry wind

Storm clouds cluster sill and shelf
hover and swirl underbed

She tries to rise
to the child   who has soiled himself
or is it she   or those who speak for her

Abed again by noon   stew pot sink rotten
Fear so broods her   dishevels
her mattress   nitty with infestation

bitten by invisibilities
she swells and claws at
itch and bleed

Neighbors are elsewhere
Youth and frolic   elsewhere
She wants to smooth her patchwork cover

stitching loose   historic colors faded
each shrunken strip   square   star
and log unfurled   filthy batting

She wants to stray   green   downhill
wants hips to unlatch   feet to arch to pink
wilding   wants yes to uncrust her lids

Oh to be wide upon a good
earth   she is loath to
turn from her bedrock and valley

She beseeches a rankled
raw-mouthed and wit-bound god
so embedded he is in her girl heart

She cannot shake loose her father's kindness
her mother knee-deep in prayer to bulb and mulch

Her unused breasts   have gone sudden tender
milk longing   nipples raw   unrooted   if only
soft lips would suckle   and defuse her

III

Bluff Path and Meadow

One, then two
fawns, snow speckled
tails ashudder
with grass joy
and their mother
look up from green feast
but do not scatter.

Blessed brown fur beasts.
Blessed the field that feeds them.

In every pine bough
a crow warns against appetite.

I am mere
biped walking
to erase nightmare.

A dragonfly settles on a stalk of purple grass.

Dry weeds shake their catch of hollow fish.
Sun shifts and they are unlit lanterns.

Flick flick, say tall grasses.

Wish upon me, whizzes the dragonfly,
frenzied to ignite another passerby.

Who wouldn't be on fire on a day prismed
and song-bellowed as this?

Follow behind, says mother deer.
Play Leap Low Bushes, say the fawns

but I am trail-tied, clumsy
among outdoor sleepers—

novice at being among
novice at being lit.

A Holiness, Nut Lush Smoke

When my father settled with a sigh into the brown plaid chair, when he pulled the ottoman closer, he had already stacked medical journals on the floor, already set his pipe in the glass ashtray and the can on the small pine table.

There was a silver clasp on the tobacco can's lid that swerved round its track like a lizard. Caught, twisted, and pressed, it popped open, and from that tin emerged bitten plums, bright summer, wet leaves, wind on the lake.

He would knock old ash and tobacco from his pipe and pinch a new feed of weedy leaves and twigs into its bowl. He struck a match on the side of a tiny matchbox set in a pewter cover and drew in the jib's release, the mainsail's swell, my mother's blue suit with silver buttons, my own sweaty forehead he'd diagnosed feverish the night before.

Then, his gaze out the long windows overlooking high pines; the hammock hung between the two straightest trunks; the still swing on its ragged ropes and the lone gull cruising calm water. Inhalation. Exhalation. Smoke trailing from his mouth, drifting over his glasses, over his wavy auburn hair, over the back of the chair. Then he set the pipe down and picked up a journal to catch up on all there was to know.

"Anything you're passionate about," he'd say, "is a life study." And he would leave us, my brother and me, his busy wife, and dip into untested theory, suggested cure, a curious disease.

That room was infused with holiness: time, reverie, and nut lush smoke.

"Science," he said, "is a blending of all the arts." Once, twice, he looked out, refilled, relit his pipe, puffed, pondered, returned to the page.

If a Man Can Teach His Daughter

after *Leaning into the Wind: Andy Goldsworthy*

to split a reed

insert
another slimmer
reed into the hollow tip

to repeat

and hang these
like icicles from limbs
above a stream

If crouched by the stream
the man rests one
hand in his daughter's lap

while she wraps wet red
leaves around each of his fingers

his other hand
already bandaged clumsily

by the hand now held
grown useless

If stream waters
striped by reeds'
shadows
redden with
elm's refuse

If the bank holds
daughter and father

if she makes of his hand
art he has taught her

is it   leaf
hand or water
that binds them

and which becomes
more beautiful
in the making?

Return with Me to Swamp of Summer

It will be March   Friday   late afternoon
The long field behind the house snow-rippled
and the pasture beyond empty

I will lift the barbed wire for you
Belly flat to snow   Crawl through
then lift it for me

Already the cows have gone to the barn
leaving snow dotted with dung and mud
Our mittens already ice-clustered

Already the sky is purple   one crow   no wind
Trudge in my tracks to the woods' edge
woods once spackled glare   skitter and buzz

It is winter

Take my hand to keep from falling
I will push back the low limbs
You   watch for the fox

Violet gold haze   crunch of boots
Fallen limbs   iced moss   mouse tracks and rabbit

We are close   there—
The Three Witch Stumps!
There—Great Clawed Fir! And there!
clearing   snow thick and dimlit—

swamp of summer
swamp of murk and croak
buzz and gurgle

But it is winter

Surely there's ice beneath the snow
Surely if we clear a path our boots can skate across
Step   with me

edge   yes   farther   take my
Oh! slush to knees   falling   we
tug each other
shivered
to shore
grin-bright
ice-plunged
heart-pound
happy

Return

past rabbit tracks

Great Fir

Three Stumps

back through

pasture
snowfield
snowfield

dusk to
dark

A Bird in the Bush

Once   upon a crimson wing   a bead of rain
and so the girl who loved beads and birds
reached beneath the dripping branch
waited for wind to toss its perch
and drop the body

into her outstretched palm—
palm she'd heaped with twigs
thistledown and gold grass—

Her other hand reached into her pocket
to pull   button   clothespin   shell
to clear debris   to make a second home   in case the first failed
pocket become cage and cave

She craved the red wing's twitch
the neck's pulse   beak's knife tip
its quick silence   sudden cry

What did the girl know of Wild Need   Flight and Song?
She was so carefully tucked in   fed and kept
busied with lessons taught by men
doused with dusted shelves and made beds
her mother: good   and quiet

And yet   and yet
she wondered where Want led

and that day decided that if she housed it—
ruby crest   wing sheen   nervous forked feet
as she was housed
she could rule it

Like a Fall Tree, a Woman

is given slim time to be
spectacular   mind clear
hair ravished with sheen

As the ash tree
flaunts its curry-gold crown
rears into day

a woman flames
abundant with offerings
Feet grip earth

pith and sapwood
heartwood and eloquence—
she is flare   and collapse

Narrowed by freezing nights
base burnished with
curling decay

she is mulch
ruddy mist   more spirit
than body

Cottonwood

I too want what's unlikely—

a Beloved to speak to
near home   a chosen one
to believe in

Daily I greet the cottonwood
I've watched grow from weed to majesty

Morning, Bright Buds

Morning, Your Green Grace   or

Good day to you, Hail-Shattered.
I'm sorry your dress is ruined.

As fall peaks   I spin by calling out
Oh you Golden Sheen Shimmer Spectacle!

> That's a bit much, Barbara, calls the tree.
> One adjective will do.

Can I call you Copper Crunch?
Can I say Bronze Bounty?   I pause and touch her side

> I like Crunch. I'm all itch and shrink
> these days before winter.

I have a Beloved I whisper   walking past

Once she is bare   once the sidewalk is iced
and snow rests in her crevices
I stop   look up

Oh I say *Oh you are gauzy and godlike!*

Often she sleeps through my winter greeting
but sometimes she creaks a reply

  And you my faithful friend
  beware hyperbole!

But I know by the way she cracks one knothole
and drops a brittle branch at my feet
She likes the company

  She says
    Your cheeks are polished apple! robin breast! chokecherry!

    Now I must nap and I know I know apple is a cliché . . .

She blows cold breath on me
I pick up my red-booted pace

And Yet I Wept

Dead oak   wide as a horse is long
its hollow black as char   as if a boy
had been dared to torch and flee

I wanted hum and
buzz like a hook

to pull me into its grotto of rot
to flare a lost hymn

mulch shimmed   elbow deep   I
leaned my ear to its clock

How green the winter breeze

how absent of sheep the slope on which the tree carcass spread

When my arm stuck   I was afraid
bees would cluster flesh
afraid

I'd be forced to accept godliness

But swallows that swept past were not bees
nor cloud over the hill   clock
nor roots creased with lichen   hymn

Nothing came of it.
A net of gray moss brushed my cheek.

Morning by the Meadow

Austerlitz, New York

I sit in the house of many windows. Scratchings in walls and rafters.

In every landscape, curtains lift, sway, and still. There is always a choice: to be kind, to be cruel. Goldenrod feathers morning mist and this new place, its elms and maples, its high grasses. Tripod in the garden empty of beans.

The teacher writes beside the student. The Irish poet is dead. No panther in the brush. No wren at the table. I am old. I am not old. Red flush to the sumac. Crickets forget themselves. I am inside. I am out. My death is this white sky.

Andrew Wyeth painted the river, tinsel uncoiling through field, mountain, slate hill. From an aerial view it is abstraction, map of a man's meandering mind. Rivulet, delta, stream, daybreak, dusk: a rendered world—Seamus Heaney's *coil and gleam of your furrowed brain.*

We wend our way in the dark, hands out to sense shifts in temperature. Squint-eyed, half asleep, we refuse the great sorrows that hold our lessons. We strong-arm what might gentle us.

I have come from canyon, thin air to heavy, to pray. Deer curl into wet grass mats. Beavers, slicked down and danced out. Emblem, object, archetype.

In childhood landscape I am bereft yet eager. I empty grit and gravel from my shoes, pull stones from between my toes. My arid home is half home. And this, half foreign. Clover. Black-eyed Susan. Queen Anne's lace. As a girl I oiled chestnuts on the side of my nose. The gleam pleased me, my pockets packed like squirrel cheeks.

Mist is my reverie, my shawl. When it rains in my high-desert home, when it snows, when clouds pile silver and black explosions, I am happiest.

My dad could skip a stone six leaps. He taught me to choose smooth ovals, but my wrist snapped too early. He said, "Teaching has a ripple effect." When he taught me to sail he snapped the lines, then blundered the jib, scowled at my clumsy hands. I have a history of *less than.*

Flat on my stomach in white-pink clover, I studied bees.

If I sit long enough a deer will cross, meadow to lawn.
It will step lightly, dew between hooves.
Cloven, cleave, taste
of wet clover.

1972

Sun plumped her smoke-wreathed cheeks
exhaled and choked day's end

Her rhinestone tiara tossed
and slid under Golden Gate.

High and nothing to do with
all   the time   We had

come for explosion and dying
Shift at Suicide Anonymous done

Embroidered with rainbows
jeans slung low. Banking on eternity
whole wheat   avocado and sprouts.

Saved a black and white pup
told him *Stay* but he as sun
slipped away—

Charms baked in each loaf *Surprise!*
Peasant blouses   loose breasts
Bell bottoms rubbed raw on sidewalks as we

waited in line for a scoop of mocha chip
waited for the sun to swing its second-hand sombrero
to unspool its vintage sweater patterned with reindeer.

Dressed for Nowhere On Time we
did not record or post   chat send or text.

We hung ferns above the tub   frescoed
ceilings with angels and lightning.

War went on.   Plague inched into lungs.
Boys we loved changed their minds.   Sometimes

our parents called and asked.   We sang
whatever Divine Miss M sang
as the boys we loved changed.

Spread oats honey and seeds on pans
jars labeled Crunch.   Sometimes
our parents asked   our meager jobs—

Until smoke
until fern tips burned
paint bubbled and burst

the dog ran and the ridiculous car
died in traffic   We kicked its tires

and fled
east where we'd come from
or south

Good-bye bridge Good-bye sun slipping under tide
Good-bye mattress and crate beside
Good-bye stitches and high
sometimes   our parents

Neighbor

A dozen years ago it was twinkling lights strung fence to porch roof
and a clawfoot tub the matriarch of the commune
sang from on summer nights

The tub is long gone   Her song
replaced by prayer flags and ruined cars
Autumn   she hunches to rows of peppers and corn

Winter now and wind is fierce

Bleached to coral and antique rose
flag tatters rail and twist
from the tip of the dying elm

Daily the woman lets one slow dog out
lets the other in   Her white hair
flies from under her red hat

Six abandoned beehives mark the lot line
Tipped into tumbleweed and cactus
painted in pastel layers

They could be graves
They might be named   *Piracy of Peace*
Ghost Town of Bitter Honey

This morning the flags quiver   rest
less flux and fury   they herald
no battle against

A coyote limps the field
The neighbor's windows are dark
Dawn claims frail tints her own

IV

Morning

Brown bread, beets in black soil,
leaven and lead sky.
We are in repose.

Morning unfolds
her kerchief
blows into its sail

clouds smooth as udders
that paunch and sag.
You can fit your pale hand

round this untouched hour
its tug like a sack
blown open

about to spill its bees.

Dnipropetrovsk

I wake in the night craving milk
and a soft voice hushing my hunger.

In dream my cheek
rests against a blue-lined breast.

It is my father's side of the family
that has the opalescent skin.

Soft skin that burns easily.
Veins near the surface—

Dnieper's delta into
the Black Sea

I inherited longing
for river and region
so distant in the past

no one can pronounce
its name

I Carry Dnieper's Dark Current

shore and forests
black loam   sky
of torn tents

infants clinging to
breasts of dead mothers
gag and claw of dirt breath in dirt beds

Torah   pissed on   remade into
shoes   these are my people
The despicable

Stealers of commerce and art
threat of threats   hissed at   spat on
vein of dread   vein of extinction   thread to the Black Sea

Gathered   *for work*
we were led   midst sap and heat
maple and birch—

I am the mother who thrashed
against the soldier
who laughed

threw me to forest floor
on pine needles and oak leaves
that are girlhood

threw me   or she   or who made me
gun against   belt into   ripped waist to ankle
while my son watched

while somewhere my unborn daughters
his gloved hands on

How was my great   or great-great   me or she
able   upright   to stumble
to the sunlit ridge

wildflowers   gully of rainwater
ravine of fresh turned soil
new grass   clover and

she fell back on
and the boy soon into
It was summer
and I became   and she   and my people
lank blossoms dug up   heaped roots   shriveled

I come from
        blue flag   May flower   bloodroot

from reed grass
                alder   linden and buttercups

from village
                become family name—
                                my Shesensky
                                                my Sissonsky
                                                                my Sisson
my emigrated
and my never to be written into the Book of

or buried alongside
in Dnipropetrovsk   in Minsk   in Boston

I carry black water

Hebrew I Cannot Read

When I sit in synagogue
I am tongue-tied   bereft
Ancient letters dissolve and morph

I decipher its alphabet   *alef beit*
    brick   buckle   gate   pendulum
    fence   table   chair

Instead of prayer   I read
    egret   serpent   tent
Instead of chant and midrash
    flame   wind   pasture

I cannot *daven*
I cannot memorize the death prayer
nor the one for waking

Stones beneath letters meant to link
consonants to music
I cannot count

I make of the alphabet a village of huts
    bridge   gate   windows
    coop   cauldron   hearth

There are hands pressed to every pane of glass
Beneath each house   feet scrape
In each guttural sound   shingle   boot   mud

It may be true they dug beets   ate borscht and
tore challah   that candles dripped as they were blessed
that wine was sipped from the dented goblet I hold
that in language I cannot master   they sang

yet I am dyslexic in inheritance
I am my mother's irritation—
        Why not in English we can understand?

There is a glass finger called a *yad*
my daughters slid under each line of Torah
I stood aside   not one among

These letters are kindling without my mouth's flame
avenue of crumbling brick   dying vines
zoo of llamas and serpents and teeth

I want to be a girl wandering a rebus
of my making   unashamed   unjudged
    lute   chisel   drum   branch   spine   knife

There is my father's pipe
mother's mallet   my brother's birdcage
There is my aunt's shovel   grandmother's candlesticks
my father's stethoscope   my mother's shears

    staff   labyrinth   kiss   bird track   ice   clapperless bell

There is the scowl of the girl who thought I had horns
Sneer of the one who said *nose so big her thumb goes all the way up*
Manna   manger   savior   they said I stole

I named my daughters
Beth: house   door   roof   bed
Elana: tree   bright shining   lover of stars

Dialect of daughters   family glyphs
ancient texts dusty on shelves—

and still my name means   *stranger*   *do without*

Vertigo with Lilacs

A split-rail fence, sun-blanched and swayed
is comfort, is handrail
is *Just in case.*

I walk the Taos road—burn barrels thinned to copper lace.
Mourning doves moan. Magpies nitpick and overspeak.
The apricot tree, witch-fingered and flammable.

Lilacs have gulped the small rains—
heads bent to passersby, purple plumes eavesdrop,
trade for gossip, pungence that swallows fear.

Antlers frame DO NOT ENTER
Scab-red with corrosion, twisted
barbed wire bares its teeth.

A majestic cottonwood is dead.
Tresses raised in perpetual alarm as if
candelabra minus wicks and wax—double menorah
my mother did not place in any window.

The tree's limbs imprint on sky
ayin   *nun*   *shin*   loosely meant:
when the earth cries

Lilacs bob and blacken.

A rusted bell is still.

In the Village Shesensky, Shabbat Out of Time

Soon I will sit with my grandmother. And her mother. And hers. A simple meal. The weather is dank, the table set with heavy plates and cloth napkins, its center yet candleless. Outside—dog, rooster, wind. Who are the men? Who are the children with jam-smeared mouths? And how does a strain of music enter under the door like a dust wisp?

Beside the stove, stacked wood. On the stove, copper pots with long-handled spoons stirring themselves. Aproned, rose-cheeked, pressed against her hip, I want to be taught which knife is best for vegetable, which for meat, and how to hold it, how to axe turnip and fowl the way my grandmother does.

Piles of beets and potatoes—onion, garlic, parsley. Meat in a pot. What kind? Whose cow or sheep? Who knows these things? And who slaughtered it? Did it come wrapped in paper and string or rolled here straight from the butcher's bloody hands? Was it blessed?

My great-grandmother is short and sturdy. Her mother is spry and busy. Am I phantom or present day, ghost or girl, thread or shawl? No one's fingernails are clean. Soil, blood and broken nails. Who dug the beet? Who pulled parsley? Who told the tale that set me down into sleep:

 of the house with chicken legs and the dybbuk keening beneath
 Nothing good nor G–d will come of this   Nothing true and nothing new
 Pull the turnip   turn the fiddle   light the wick   Oh nothing good will come of this

No wonder we are tired. No wonder we are ravenous.

Rain spatter and cease. Sun is stretched and squeezed between village roofs like a latke crowded into a skillet and pressed to oil. Sparks fly. Crows, released from their convent, soar and bark.

We are hungry. We are always hungry. My grandmother is a girl beside me. She whispers and we giggle. Her red hair tickles my cheek. Time to slap and braid the dough. My hands and her hands. Another grandmother says, *Easy now.* Slap   pummel   stretch. My grandmother tugs her braid of dough and I tug mine and my great-great-grandmother threads her third slippery rope, wraps and pats.   *Shabbat   Shabbat   Shabbat shalom*   Wisp of song from the river's opposing bank. Soon it will be over, day of wine the color of beets, day of yeast.

Surely we will never leave this stone house. We will sleep in these rumpled beds and spoon stew and kill chickens. We will wait— for snow for ruin and monsters and sun. We will wait for thieves horses rope. Our nights thickened by rough woven blankets, we will dream in rooms where a mouse scurries but no rat.

Always I am a girl in a stone house uphill from Dnipropetrovsk. My uncles are boys sprouting whiskers and magic tricks. Town of brick dust and prayer. Shul of men, yarmulke and tallit. Shul that beckons and refuses. Pews of moth and moan, paraffin, dust, and wool.

Tomorrow we will go to Dnieper's dark curve and visit the graves. Riverbank of gather and gunshot. River of floating birch bark and buttercups. River of sails and oars and depths I am not afraid of. It will be summer and we will spread a blanket with what was not eaten last night. Blessings and wildflowers. Spoons to clack and pots to turn into drums. Ribbons thrown to wind and caught back to wrist.

> *Fancy that,* my great-grandmother hums from a stump of ash. Suddenly young, she has gathered blown willow branches and wound them with grass, made a switch, a broom.
> *Fancy that,* she sings. *And did you know?* she leans close.
> *Baba Yaga swept away her tracks with a broom such as this and off you go!*
> She grins and shoos us with a swish. We are half joy, half afraid.

My great-great-uncle says,

> *History is a cow and a copper pot*
> *Though newly polished it is pocked with a hundred hungers*
> *Though milked and returned to pasture*
> *it is slow to remember where the fence is barbed.*

Exile Song

Stories of how we fled and
how we survived revive in spring—

how all skin burns   how common our thirst   how absent the angels
how infused with grit   dust and salt   food
stolen or begged   or made en route

Some crawl through cactus   blister and shrink toward safe haven
Some crowd inflatable boats   certain a frigid sea is overseen by saints

My people's forty years was a freedom pact   fed by thin scripted tablets
Pocked unleavened bread so dry on the tongue
some gagged and spat it out

And those whose unknown ancestors did the fleeing
settle around a table and sing   or for weeks fast and pray
or heft a cross upon their backs and walk uphill to somewhere holy

In spring   we say   *Look—the lilies' green ears push through dirt!*
We say   *Already the child knows the word for milk!*

The angels rattle their snow-crusted wings   revile silence and forgetting
The angels are cynics and wise women   pagan and prophet
sickened by our mute tongues   our fisted hearts

They want to tug us from stupor   send us back to where story began
back to Pharoah and dictator   drug lord   traitor   sellers of souls
back to holy men   mystics   and texts writ to save us

Slap go the wet cold wings   The angels
grow exhausted with our vague rituals and tight lips

But it is spring—   *See the apple tree's pale bud?*
Look, the child can climb stairs to the porch!

Some of us shake parsley in salt water   say *Tears and hope*
watch matzo balls swell and float   bite horseradish to know bitterness
crush apples and nuts to cement a house

Some of us take the infant mouth to breast and hum
what a grandmother hummed   add a verse
adjust the tune to suit this morning—

in every language   an exile song
in every land a beaten path littered
with torn pages   lost shoes   belts and bodies

It is spring—surely a miracle will surprise us
Surely memory will be turned from feral to feast

Angels will swarm and lean into each retold tale
wings shedding ice and their tongues
soft against their teeth

V

Aftermath

While I Search the Divine

The bees in the bacopa
dive white bloom to bloom
up to their striped hips
in nectar and November light.
These wild-eyed
flit-and-feed machines
show how it is done—

head first, upside down
into what opens
legs flail, ankles cross,
gravity lost, they
headstand within
white trumpets
gulp, reverse, and
whir delirious.

How else get to the bottom
where it's had time
to thicken and turn
dangerously sweet?

Night Yard

You can have any flower you want
though if you pluck it the penstemon will no longer ring its bells.

Take the coreopsis. True, its green feathers
will rash the hands. Its bright suns shrink at your touch.

And roses, pale as antique linen—
frail layers will break in an open palm.
Close your hand or the breeze will rob you.

Dear sweetling, I call the black dog
as we turn our heads to stars.

The Dipper pours her milk over the dog's back;
she's suddenly star freckled and frisky.

Three a.m., garden disappeared by night rebels
but our feet steady on invisible earth.

Do not forget the lover
who sleeps through your going out
and coming in.

Dream with Goats and Boy

The goats broke through the garden wall
five or six   big as ponies   And the boy ran after
in the field   there was a hole
narrow as his shoulders
feet first   he arrowed into

Goats the color of dust
jaws set   eyes terrified
The wall crumbled   stucco and rebar
heaped into rubble   There had been
so many pictures of war

The boy was thin   clad in gray
a pole   he became   a disaster
he was running from
and the hole seized his ankles
It might once have been a well
or dug for a post
or a conduit for power

The goats' breath   the color of howling

The wall was meant
to hold the garden and its
small table   its two metal chairs

This is a dream
yet

I heard the stone birdbath crack
a clay saint shatter
a dog fight its chain

The goats came as a rampage
become a kind of pillage

You know   how one thing
leads to another

I look out
every morning
to see if the wall
stands

Mayhem of Piñon Jays

Limbs glint with sap
No cloud   no wind

A hundred jays
blast the piñon

Shot through with silver
their sunlit wings mercurial
brassy bird-fish flip and twist
limn black boughs metallic
    —shiver of glass shards
        : azure quiver
                no sky can mimic

These seasonal thieves
are knives that pierce
and ransack

any opening

burst cones
nuts easy to beak
and steal

In aftermath

tremble

a hundred broken rooms
Blue feathers snagged by bark
Shaken needles curl in heat

What hoarded seeds the jays do not retrieve
may sink into soil
may sprout

Stillness

the second siege

Flinch Tunnel Cradle

Rats tunnel under the long-limbed cholla
Its ancient octopus legs grind into piñon needles

It is easy to axe and collapse hollow cactus branches
It is not easy to deter the feral hunkered beneath

nor to remain free of bristles and blood

        When the massage therapist presses
        tangled nerve and muscle I flinch

Always night when the skunk gasses its enemy
Pungence and protection waft our rooms

To bunker is to make of a tunnel haven
Often—illusion of safety

        Elsewhere my daughter grows a child
        Her belly the half-moon I stand beneath
        Her belly the ladle I dip into soup

                When in the dark he
                surprises me with tenderness
                I flinch relent allow happiness

        In every photo she texts
        her hands cradle her belly
        and I cradle mine

The moon—segment of citrus
punctured by autumn leaves tart juice
I slurp The dog licks my chin

Hope   I say and she
with her tail   agrees

In spring there will be cholla flowers
pink waxy cups   bees will clamor and
thrashers will fill the prickly V's with nests

Post-op Umbilical Hernia | | Record Heat in High Desert | | Rivers Flood Northeast

Not to remove but relieve
pain and swell   he is punctured

Three incisions where once
cord to mother curled

Sealed with mesh fine as fly wings
Blue then orange   then underripe lime   his bruises

Collectors of sunsets and bird calls we
repeat the towhee's three-note treble capped with riff

Once birds did not need our basins of water
nor rain our prayers   nor slow rivers to be staunched

Grasses now tinder   once were fodder
Rivers once paddle and meander   ransack banks

Nine p.m.   July heat less searing   slowly   stiff
and healing he and I walk the dog

Home   my husband allows me   wincing
flinches as I touch   glued and shaved flesh

We pray   recovery without flare or fluvial impediment
My cheek scrapes bristled slope   rests on sweat-slick shore

Silt and Bone

Not buried
my parents
glide among lakeweed

rattle with incoming tide—
their bone bits
rub against

the dock ladder
pocked with rust
rough with corrosion

they cede this life
for a next

Caught by
tree roots that reach
shore to sandy bottom

Overseen by mallard
and geese   dragonflies
skim above

Jewish custom is not
to burn a body but coffin and
place dry rocks upon a headstone

As tradition would not
have it   my parents
drift and settle

Particulate   they animate
the cold clear lake they loved
with no hope   to reincarnate

but company they keep—
trout   pond weed   turtle   eels
is congregation

and lake bottom that shifts
shrinks and heaves
is belief

Let them be
sediment   continuance
and underwater song

May deer lap edges of their forever
and grandchildren
swim among

Late Fragments

with lines from Dionne Brand's "Thirsty"

How badly we need
to turn daily affairs
toward the marvelous.

Hannah Weiner, poet-clairvoyant
sees words on her forehead.
I cannot axe my angels.

I am innocent as thresholds

I imagine God
blue-gray cloud wisp, thin as vapor
serious as the unwritten page.
Also a well: padlocked to protect from drowning.

Who is scribe and
who bedeviled supplicant?
Who did I love more than myself?

The touch of everything blushes me
Pigeons and wrecked boys
. . . this embrace with broken things

Orange shadow on brown stucco.
Sun weeping toward sleep.
We leave day
kindled and lit.

Enough has been done.

If you do not hear the sheep, I understand.
It has taken years for their moans and bleats to reach me.
Years to understand their deliberate chewing.
How their small feet, their sad eyes
guide them to grass.

In the Immediacy: Late Prayer

Loose the drawstring so I am freed
and newly kin with all that is outer and green laden
all that is boulder and fine sand   heat blister and frozen
root dark and hoary frost flick.   Press me flush with the world I lust after.

Never molded to my limbs and flesh enough—this wilderness
this jungle of vines and tendrils   animal breath and soughing in pines.
Flesh of my flesh—said but not meant. Otherwise wouldn't I
be impregnated with heart of hare and horse   toad and tarantula?
Wouldn't I be skin to skin with rain-drenched leaves and sodden bark?

Uncallus me to permit the flood of other in.
Make of me a porous seepage.   Make of my feet   hoof   fin   claw.
That there be oozing back and forth   that sap
become sweat to glisten elbow   hip   knees

That I might flip and flail into juicing bodies—
sister swamp   scummed pond.
Field broken by harrow   cut brittle   shorn:
I will syrup and sop that field.

Strip me skinless to become one with stream   cloud   shore.
Render me animal to inhabit free roamers and stabled.
Teach me to speak in growl   hoot   and cough of ice-cut wind.
Deep in my nostrils—wolf mist   hare twitch   mule whinny.

Microscopic   I will swim with what will kill and what will save us.
Bandage me with hide of beasts that died and beasts that live.
Blood of my blood   Mold me to the shape of flood
that I be river's horrible swell   that I learn *surge.*

Volcanic   crush every bone and organ
that I become one with torched rock   that molten and malleable
I roil and purge and am the pouring guts.

Shrink me to flea   to milkweed fluff   to wheeze and hush.
Snap my laddered spine to spinelessness so I might be blown to sky.
Scatter me   over and through   earth's breath and breathless things.

Night said

Acknowledgments

These poems previously appeared in the following publications:

"Dear sweetling" in my poem "Night Yard" is inspired by Brigit Pegeen Kelly's poem "Blessed Is the Field," in which she uses the phrase "Lonely Sweetling."

ABQ InPrint: "Home Meadow," "Neighbor"

Bosque, the journal: "Girl with Red Scarf, Dreamt Tale" (contest finalist)

Cirque: "New Year's Beside the Playa"

Glissando!: "Near Acre of Home," "If a Man Can Teach His Daughter," "High Summer's Thin Wrist"

Hobart: "Raft Dress, Refugee"

The Minyan: "Erev Shabbat, I Become Matriarch"

Notes of Light and Dark: Southwest Aubades and Nocturnes: "Disturbed Pastoral"

The Santa Fe New Mexican Pasatiempo: "Bread in the Time of COVID-19"

The Santa Fe Reporter: "Night Yard" (contest winner)

Spiral Orb: "God in the Lesser Nighthawk"

Split Rock Review: "Snowstorm with Lament"

Stone Gatherings: "Bread in the Time of COVID-19" (reprinted)

Telepoem Booth Collected Calls Anthology: "If a Man Can Teach His Daughter"

The Unruly Muse Podcast: "Girl With Red Scarf, Dreamt Tale," "There was pause"

Writing Through the Apocalypse: Pandemic Poetry and Prose: "There was pause"

For Sadie, dog of deep spirit.

Many people have supported and inspired the creation of these poems. Thank you to those who have read and offered perspective and encouragement—the MHFC: Meghan Adler, Terry Blackhawk, Jolynn Free, Katherine Gekker, John Gualtieri, Nancy Hechinger, Frances Jo Grossman Kennedy, Bia Lowe, Kate McGloughlin, Ivana Mestrovic, Judy Michaels, and Katherine Williams; my longstanding and wise poetry group: Tina Carlson, Debby Casillas, Robyn Hunt, Donald Levering, Mary F. Morris, and the late Gary Worth Moody; and the blessed Flamingos: Sandra Hunter,

Marcia Meier, Tania Pryputniewicz, Lisa Rizzo, Ruth Thompson, Michel Wing, and Barbara Yoder.

Thank you to Marie Howe for mentorship and friendship, and to Lise Goett for inspirational teaching and finding the thread and themes of this book.

Kyce Bello, muse and soul mate in the divining of poems—her wonder and adventurous spirit inspire my own.

I am indebted to Claire Lichtenstein for long friendship and deep conversation about faith and ancestry. Her entry into and passion for my poems is a rare gift.

My students and the New Mexico poetry community offer a spirit of literary camaraderie that I will never take for granted.

I am most grateful to University of New Mexico Press, especially Elise McHugh and Hilda Raz, for their enthusiasm and commitment to the Mary Burritt Christiansen Poetry Series. Thank you to Richard Lehnert for meticulous copyediting.

Thank you to Janet Russek for her generosity and enthusiasm in sharing her photograph from the Wheelbarrow Series, "Swirl With Pine Cones," as the cover of this book.

For the gifts of place—northern New Mexico, New England, Oregon, Ireland, Northern California—landscapes and their inhabitants, animal, plant, and weather, that held and hold. I am grateful to live among them and translate what I can. Atlantic Center for the Arts, Cliffs of Moher Retreat, Millay Arts, and Playa at Summerlake have offered gifts of time and mentorship.

Rick, Elana, and Beth, my beloved cheerleaders, I love you.

About the Author

Barbara Rockman is the author of *Sting and Nest,* winner of the New Mexico–Arizona Book Award and the National Press Women Book Prize; and *to cleave,* finalist for the International Book Award and winner of the National Press Women Book Prize. Her award-winning poems appear in numerous journals and anthologies.

Barbara has taught at Santa Fe Community College, Renesan Institute for Lifelong Learning, and in community workshops. She was the workshop coordinator for Wingspan Poetry Project, bringing poetry to victims of domestic violence; the poetry coordinator for OutsideIn Arts, developing poems with people living with mental illness; and is a workshop facilitator for the Voice Project, creating space for unhoused populations to tell their stories through poetry. She is the founder of Santa Fe's Community of Voices, a music, poetry, and prose reading series; and co-curator of Poets@ HERE, a poetry reading series.

Barbara earned her MFA in Writing at Vermont College of Fine Arts. She grew up in the Berkshire Hills of western Massachusetts and lives in Santa Fe, New Mexico.

